Parentheses { }

Parentheses { }

HELEN LEPP FRIESEN

RESOURCE *Publications* · Eugene, Oregon

PARENTHESES { }

Resource Publications
An Imprint of Wipf and Stock Publishers
199 W. 8th Ave., Suite 3
Eugene, OR 97401

www.wipfandstock.com

PAPERBACK ISBN: 978-1-5326-0183-5
HARDCOVER ISBN: 978-1-5326-0185-9
EBOOK ISBN: 978-1-5326-0184-2

Manufactured in the U.S.A.   NOVEMBER 30, 2016

For Daniel, Andrew, Emily, David, and Timothy

Contents

Contents

Introduction

Parentheses { } is a collection of poetic observations about life's taxonomy, where I wonder what is real - the life I live when I am awake or the life I live in my dreams. Sometimes the limitation of my understanding of this world with its many layers and shadows overwhelms and humbles me to a deep sense of appreciation for the simultaneous simplicity and complexity of the physical and spiritual world. With heuristic methods, I ponder on life's mystery as I yearn for a place of being fully awake. I wonder about the irony of different definitions of riverfront property; I mourn the loss of missing children; I wonder about visible and invisible boundaries, gates, and walls.

Each poem is accompanied by another extension poem in parentheses. Often we treat script in parentheses as optional, as something that didn't quite fit into the regular text but was vying for inclusion nonetheless. The lines in parentheses in this case are integral to the poem, just like our subconscious mind is integral to our consciousness, just like one season quietly leans on the previous one as it slips into the next with but a gossamer film in between.

Parentheses { } takes the reader on a journey through the four diverse seasons in both nature and human life. In a circular algorithmic pattern, we as sojourners on this earth experience beginning end, birth death, springtime harvest, sunrise sunset, but with each gyroscopic rotation, the view changes. These poems are about meeting God and ourselves on life's trajectory, in the eyes of our children, in the face of complete strangers, in disillusionment and despair, in paradoxes, in goodbyes, and in harmony.

PART 1

Spring

BROWN EYED SUSAN (RUDBECKIA TRILOBA)

russet taffeta buttons with canary satin slippers
        he loves me
        he loves me not
        he loves me
march blissfully along gravel aisles
smooth valleys with abundant smiles
wealth in a delighted child's arm
idoneous royal wave to a casual observer
summer gold for everyone's earthly urns
until

        {once sturdy petals droop in outward frailty
        at season's turn of the page
        when
        he loves me
        settles into
        deep wrinkles of soul's depth
        faltering steps now in faded saffron satin
        until death do us part
        life in topiary lemon trees
        to be remembered in sepia photographs
        russet taffeta buttons with canary satin slippers}

PASSING THE BATON

Spring hovers on the last whispers of winter
when snow reluctantly sacrifices its shape.
Change in the wind welcomes back
Diaspora of V-shaped Canadian geese.

I buy David ubiquitous black and brown rain boots
at Goodwill.
Saturday morning
we go to Crescent Drive Park
to stomp through
stained glass ice.

  {We gather big sheets
  to play the cymbals,
  millions of crystal shards
  never to be put back together
  like a reflection of childhood all in a row.
  Sun rises high in the sky
  to gently persuade the frost
  time has come to move on
  when we trade boots for the next size.}

RAFTING IN THE SPRING

When warm spring sun
stared away obdurate snow storms, sleet
slowly melted drifts
a pond settled behind pragmatic barns
that's when the remains of winter's snow
became refuge
for eager pussy willows
jocular children
winter confined
now burst from reticent crust
to spend hours
cobbling rafts
from farm scraps
barrels, wooden planks roughly
nailed together

{sailed gloriously across winter tears
with jagged sticks for paddles
and splendid dreams for sails}

DREAMS IN FLIGHT

Daniel dreams in flight
at first small steps that stretch
to longer higher ones
until in grand leaps and bounds
he circumnavigates the world

       {his ideas sail, completely airborne
       with an occasional tap on the earth}

THE FIRST BAREFOOT

May we go barefoot
outside
we begged as soon as spring
leaned heavily on the thermometer

Not until the snow is all melted
came the annual reply

Busily we shoveled the last
tired dirt-stained snow piles
spread their cold
evenly on still dormant grass
to let the warm sun consume them eagerly

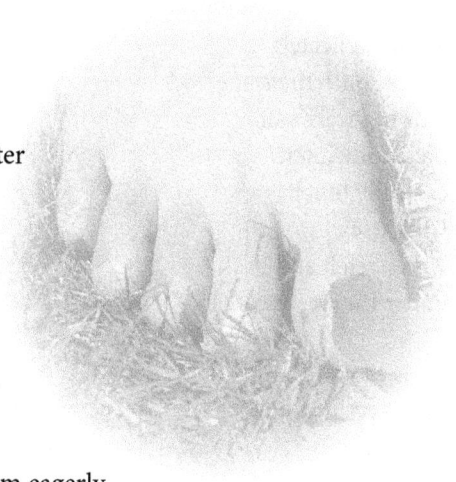

> {Then we flung the attached boots
> taciturn socks to the sky
> skipped eagerly across the grass
> digging toes into silky coolness
> rolling over and over
> exhilarating in the grand entrance of spring
> as if for the first time}

EATING WILD ROSES

Spring delicately
dances onto the stage
blowing warm air
on aloof winter,
carefully touches
wild roses
who stretch and bask
under the warm caress.

Shyly blossoms open
their eyes to squint
at the sun.

{My sisters and I gently pick
fragile pale pink petals
savor their sweet flavor
determined to become one with spring.}

SEIZE THE INNOCENCE

of stranded childhood
embracing each minute

> {with the awareness
> that temporary islands
> are cairns to eternal continents.}

PLANTING A GARDEN

Placing dry shriveled seeds into black soft earth
comes with eternal hope
preparation of life so tedious
and time-consuming
furrowing straight rows on days and months
gathering choice seeds of virtue
for the spring banquet
carefully selected
corn, carrots, and beans

      {depositing hope in a grave
      to see it sprout
      innocent in its green youth
      wise in its maturity
      delicious in a harvest feast}

BANANA NUT BREAD ANYONE?

She walks the flea market's dusty path
carrying a baby in a car seat
in the other hand
a basket of small loaves.

Banana nut bread anyone?

Etched in her melancholy eyes
her plaintive plea
translates her bigger burdens.

> {Ten-year-old Andrew pulls out a dollar
> and lightens her basket of
> one humble loaf.}

JUST AN ERRAND

A simple mundane walk down the street
with three-year-old David
to accomplish a tedious errand
is suddenly snatched up and recast as an adventure.

Sticky hands and nose pressed
against Roseborough and Barber law offices,
leave smudgy decorations
on the immaculate, unblemished window.

Standing rooted to the sidewalk
he admires a painter transform
the entrance of Vision Unlimited
as though that painter were Michelangelo himself
adorning the Sistine Chapel.

Caressing the adobe pillars,
even licking the rough surface,
he savors the million and one germs.

On a manhole cover
on the corner of Second and Coal
he dances a jig, thrilled by the xylophone of different tones
with each step and tap.

On the grass patch beside Sunwest Bank,
dandelion seeds beckon
where every single one

needs to be blown,
enough to seed dandelions
all over the world.

He buries his nose in the grass,
rolls and tumbles exuberantly,
with every intention of embracing that enchanted moment
and holding onto it for all eternity.
At the mention of going home, a howl of protest.

{WHY would anyone
with even a little bit
of imagination
think of ending such an exquisite journey?}

MORLEY

Daniel met Morley at a stop light, biking home from work.
Morley was biking around the continent. He started out somewhere in Texas. Circuitous destination I think Washington, DC. Their journeys intersected at the same corner in downtown Winnipeg. A conversation ensued because Morley, besides his traveling gear, sported a solar panel on his bike to charge his cell phone.

I got a call from Daniel after 5 that day. Was it okay if a fellow biker came home for dinner and to spend the night? Trustworthy because of the solar panel. Tall, lanky Morley ate dinner like the possibility of a next meal was questionable. Breakfast in the morning the same. Then they were on their way. Daniel to work downtown and Morley to Washington DC to get married.

> {Morley, if you are reading this poem, please call to let us know you got there okay. Let us know how the wedding went and the marriage. If you send me your address, I will send your red and black bike gloves, signature that you were actually here.}

A POEM FROM JAIL

On Monday morning
he hands in his poem on the other side
of an inventory slip from the county jail
that lists his inconsequential belongings: pants, shirt, and wallet

> {An artistic sculpture in its presentation
> I wonder which side of the paper represented
> the actual story he meant to tell}

MOSES

Despite broken tablets and promises
culturally appropriate golden idols
Almighty God reaches through time and space
to touch humanity then and now
with a healing hand
to
grant us a heavenly glimpse

{a reflection of the Promised Land}

WHAT IS A PRAYER?

In recognition of
a thunderstorm in upper case
an individual blade of grass tucked among millions
icicles hanging from eaves in spring's precipice
an ebb and flow of lines on a handprint
a turtledove's melancholic coo
wisps of clouds
rabbit's soft fur
aroma of baking bread
full moon rising
laughter
tunes falling into harmony and out again
waves lapping onto sandy shores
whirring of a hummingbird
a heart beating
engineering of a mosquito
warbling of a bird

  {and maybe a few words}

WHAT COLOR IS MY SOUL?

When does a soul begin or end?
Where is it housed in my earthly vessel?
What color is it?
Green like fresh shoots in the spring
Brilliant red in the rosebush of summer
Crimson in the decline of fall
White in winter's depth
Where is the door for its entrance
and a path for its exit?

> {how limited my understanding
> amidst all the acquisition
> accumulation and storage of knowledge when
> the essence of my very being
> escapes words and punctuation}

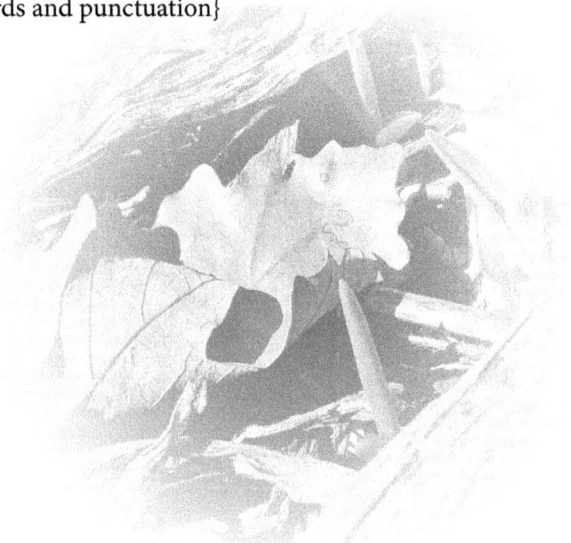

PART 2

Summer

HAPPINESS FLOWERS

fill the meadow
at the peak of summer sun
sprinkled like salt in emerald grass
among wild strawberries and sweet clover
their yellow nugget interior
encircled with enchanted delicate white lace

       {little snippets of magic
       in an everyday
       are as innumerable as happiness flowers
       on the lazy farm paddock
       if I would just open my soul}

RIVERFRONT PROPERTY

Biking trails like filigree lace
decorate the city's heartbeat
limestone path along the river
where deep foliage almost conceals
a well-established summer village
Sun peaks through windows in branches
to reveal an exclusive mysterious river front property
tents, tattered tarps cobbled to make shelters, shopping carts with muddy
wheels,
logs in a circle, fire pits
sleeping bags in calm midmorning tranquility
air etched with memories of campfire histories
without mailbox or forwarding address
tangled hair and matted clothing
slowly emerge from where the night left off
another day to gather scant belongings onto shoulders and backpacks
traverse a downtown radius
park bench naps in the sun
hot soup and sandwiches at All Saints Anglican church

{all just down the street from other riverfront properties
elegant houses
with geraniums in window boxes
where owners mow manicured Saturday morning lawns,
arrange garage sale signs on mailboxes
that collect letters with return addresses
excess possessions that do not fit in backpacks
attach flashy motorboats to powerful trucks

for far away excursions on placid lakes
beside additional lakefront cottages}

CHOKECHERRY JELLY

once upon a summer's picnic
chanced upon trees
expectant with amethyst clusters
too bitter for knowledgeable birds
succulent berries
plinked and plunked into pails
furtive secret behind skin's acerbic reputation
destined for sapid greatness

{chokecherry jelly for breakfast}

GATHERING COLORS

dusk gathers remnants of gossamer light
with fluted edges
twilight waves its magic wand
collects emerald gems from petals
dappled ivy releases its variegated blush
as night subdues lustered streets and
damask meadows
shadows snatch grape from hyacinths
ruby from velvet tapestry
suck delicious cocktail flowers
snuff out turquoise from tassels and beads
darkness gathers all colors into its supple apron

  {in safe tranquility
  waits for sunrise call
  to shake colors back into existence}

HIDE AND SEEK IN THE CORN

corn in its glorious summer peak
stands proudly row by row
brilliant green arms dance gracefully
rustling silk gently in the wind
golden spun shiny translucent hair
thrown back over an arrogant head

we play
hide and seek in this crowd
of haughty self-respecting characters
they act their roles in our game
sway delicately to hugs
caress our heads softly
tease tangled braids

we cower underneath their protection
of tassels covering us indiscreetly
with their ample thighs
not whispering our whereabouts
yet in constant conversation with each other
laughing no doubt

{about the quiet exchange of knowledge}

LAUNDRY LINE DANCE

Even laundry laughs and dances

    {when infused with imagination}

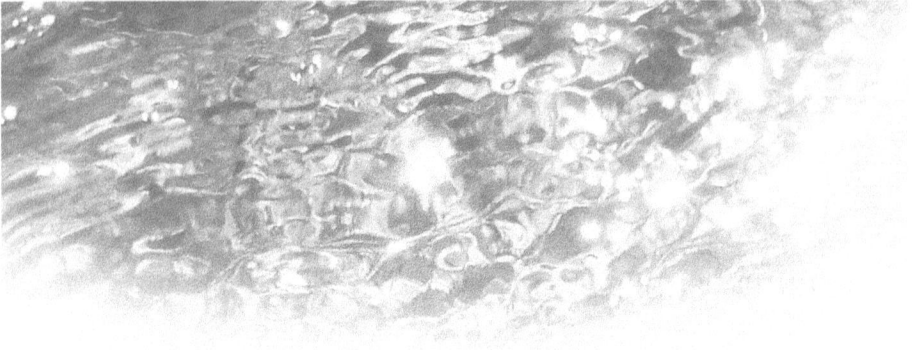

SUMMER'S END AT GRAND BEACH

Thousands of feet leave whimsical prints
in changing grains of time.

Fading warm lap of summer sun cradles stranded fish
where long fingers of mirthless water
cannot reach.

Liquid pearl streams
from setting sun
over waves and crests
until it dissolves into backdrop of eternal sand.

Chill winds chase a melancholy wail of seagulls
fluttering over meager morsels
with memories of more succulent picnics.

The beach bids farewell to reminiscence
of crystal children's laughter
faces adorned with sticky ice cream shadows
majestic sandcastles washed to mere recollections
shady silhouettes of lovers on moonlit nights.

> {Summer takes one long last deep breath
> of waves rising and falling to the beat of perpetual seasons
> before it waits expectantly
> to be clothed in winter's austere garments.}

REHABBING A QUILT

Brand new shiny spotless quilt
perfect stitches straight like
dreams all in a row
at marriage's trail head
quilt travels years
destinations
wear and tear of a relationship
tattered edges
feelings
frayed flowers
expectations
torn seams
perceptions
many fellow quilts discarded
too threadbare for repair
others
carefully sewed back together
faithful patches
patient stitches
healing sutures

{in constant preparation
for another adventure}

VELVETEEN PARASOL

A
gift from
a friend paper doll
parasol yellow and emerald
meadow lipstick roses fragile like a breakable
bird she opens closes seasons twirls around and around too
quickly tiny skeleton sticks snap wings droop sadly fix it she demands I try
but life has drained from the pretty colors I'm sorry disappointment
clouds her face suddenly eyes light she jumps up happily

{my
para
sol
has
be
come
real}

HOMELESS BALLET

There she was
her first dance lesson
white ballerina suit speckled with silver and noble goals
flawless white socks and aspirations
tucked into tiny ballerina slippers
her eyes sparkle with anticipation
shiny mirror walls
reflect her thousand images
youth, beauty, stamina, ambition pirouette
in the polished glass

Outside we scurry past eyes averted
an aged woman shuffling
on her street corner dance floor
disheveled, awkward steps with nowhere to go
eyes dull
clothes tattered
hand outstretched
to strangers' compassion
destiny so final
within the walls that suffocate her
rearview mirrors blindly
flow in the traffic of important destinations
my eyes suddenly sting

> {harsh and austere contrasts
> hurl a jagged reality in my predictable world
> where the luxury of a dance lesson for one

is for another like the next meal of daily dreams
on a contented table for now and tomorrow}

EMERALD CITY GLASSES

Driving down Highway 666
country music playing on the radio
to wile away many monotonous hours
of ribbon pavement heading straight north among
gray shrubbery greenish gray sage gray dust
a few hitchhikers to break the ennui
austere crags sprout out of the ground near Shiprock
where we look for animal shapes to keep us awake
David starts fussing to the beat of the music
and I say, "Emily, read to him."
Her reply with her nose pressed against the window,
"But Mom, I can't. I'm looking at the scenery.
It's so wonderful."

> {A creative excuse for not reading to David or
> she sees the beauty
> that I am missing that day.}

A GAME SNEAKS UP FROM BEHIND

While waiting for car repair,
a flight, in the checkout counter,
in the doctor's office, at the bus stop, for the movie to start,
for the parents to finish

> {around the corner
> a game sneaks up from behind
> expecting to be found
> to fill quiescent space}

INCONGRUENCE

Obviously the everyday bike sports the standard
two wheels
pedals
frame in a variety of commonplace and brilliant colors
assortment of usual accessories
like bells, baskets, and panniers in sundry shapes and sizes

That's why this inimitable bike
catches my senses off guard.
Instead of the usual handlebar basket
an aquarium complete with water and live gold fish swimming
happily on a field trip
Instead of a back wheel basket
tall plants in pots
growing to their hearts' motion

> {sleep and dreams
> make me wonder
> whether this bike traversed across the gossamer curtain
> and suddenly appeared in three-dimensional quality
> when I thought I was awake,
> too quickly gone to capture as photograph.}

A PROPER BURIAL

Timothy stumbled over a dead blue jay on a doorstep
while doing his paper route.
Carefully he cradled the stiff bird
placed it under a spruce tree while he dug a hole.
Solemnly he delivered the bird to the soil from whence it came,
covered it with earth, twigs, and a circle of stones in memory and ceremony.

    {Ever after when we pass that tree
    on Pheasant Bay
    we remember the blue jay
    that skipped a season.}

PART 3

Autumn

WHERE?

In unmarked graves unrecorded
children went missing
not even Missing Children posters
pasted on street signs and grocery store bulletin boards
signaled whispers of hope and expectant recovery
waiting for societal alchemy

> {walking among us still
> are families
> whose hearts are engraved with loss
> remembering the gravestones in invisible cemeteries
> national sorrow, a country at half-mast}

OUR TURN

We wait for our turn to play the game
when we have learned the rules
of language and social decorum
but not even then sometimes
do they let us

{I wonder why?}

HUMAN RIGHTS MUSEUM

Recursive sorrow
immersion of voice and experience

{polyvocality on an inimitable timeline
calls for recursive learning}

HELP

Faded and chipped paint
Work needed
austere barred windows
call delivery of workers
like packages fastened
with duct tape and email addresses
that turn the heater on at night
but fail to furnish the soul

{Apply within}

AUTUMN ACAPELLA

leaves whisper in rainbow soliloquy
refrain in thousands of voices
summer packed away

> {in neat calendar pictures
> until we meet again}

LIMITATIONS

I think my grasp
of what there is to know
in this world and beyond
is as limited
as one tiny speck
on an acorn cupule
amidst an expansive forest universe

{that continues living
without human plans
where years connect to the earth with roots
to the sky above with invisible breath
and delivers crops in precise DNA sequence
generation after generation.}

AN ABANDONED APPLE ORCHARD

On the edge of town
lives an abandoned apple orchard
where we park with permission
equipped with bags and boxes
we trip through the rusty garden gate
past the dry bird bath
gnarled unkempt trees
apples litter the ground extravagantly
from the harvest
owners failed to collect
the house now stands vacant
because the apples became too heavy

{Filling boxes to overflowing
we go home to make pie, cider
some frozen for tomorrow's muffins
unlike time that cannot be preserved
in canning jars and freezer bags.}

AN APPLE PIE IS AN ARIA

When summer lolls to an end
apple trees have collected enough memories and melodies
of crimson and gold
staccato pattered into pails
chopped into morsels

> {to fill with music
> a delicate crust baked to a melodic aria}

TIME

Demanding schedules
out of tune traffic lights
never-ending flow of email travel
leaves my soul out of breath.
I put in a requisition for more time.
Denied.

> {Time comes in peopled increments
> of the elaborate and the mundane
> sufficient for the individual journey.}

TRAJECTORY ON A TIMELINE

Her frightened and nervous eyes
on the first day of school
form the same knot in my stomach
that I remember so well
I recognize her shy glance and unsure words
when speaking with adults on cue
Her sparkling eyes at the sight of a brand new outfit
transport me back to delightful
new dress days of my childhood.
Her laughter
her freedom
beckon me across the years.

> {On this timeline of life
> I wonder where I really am
> and which one is me.}

FIRST DAY OF SCHOOL PHOTO

Snapped a first day of school photo of Timothy and Nelson
who have walked together since forever.

When I looked later
there in line stood Snowflake, the bunny,
posing for the ritual

> {just like he had also always belonged and always would,
> recorded in the family history.}

CATATONIC FEAR

Light switch on
quick heart-racing trip down gloomy stairs
into the bowels of a basement cave
past the ominous cistern
where alligators breed

another light switch on to illuminate
winter dormitory of shapeless hats, coats, skates
dangling from the wall in baggy array

a mad dash for the cold storage room
at cave's end
another light on
to the musty earthy damp potato room
errand accomplished
pail filled with summer's gifts
blood pulsing in frantic circulation

first light in succession off
a dash past the swaying wall figures
wearing strangely familiar lumpy hats and coats
next light off when

an anonymous hand upstairs
suddenly
extinguishes the last light
palpable Black so thick it breathes
its raspy breath down my neck

choking my voice to an inaudible scream
it curls its coarse fingers around arms and legs
making movement impossible
with one last strained effort
the voice box evokes a desperate screech
"Turn the light on please"
until welcome light once again floods the cave
fills the crevices with faint warmth
legs gain strength for one final attempt
race up the stairs, fling open the basement door

{to calmly deliver potatoes for dinner's menu}

LOST: ONE MOTHER

Write about the last time
you lost something, which didn't turn up
until you had replaced it or were about to replace it.
The other students wrote the usual things,
the Murphy law kind of things,
lost keys they found weeks later in the purse
a lost ring that had inconspicuously slipped in between
something unimportant in a school locker
a misplaced cd that had wandered by itself of course into a closet
a lost van in the mall parking lot
or the owner's lost memory of where she had parked the van.

Her essay, though, said
she lost her mother at birth.
Her mother left her without a name
to the care of her grandmother.
For years she had searched for her
mother's face in nameless crowds.
Could she be camouflaged under a different disguise
like lost keys in a purse?
How could a mother slip unobtrusively
between unimportant papers and books
like a lost ring in a locker?
Could she be incarcerated like a lost cd in a closet?
Or had memory just failed to reveal her whereabouts
in the anthology of faces?
One day her mother was introduced to her.
The same woman who left her without a name

was hollow vacant
not able to love.
The father dead.
I suppose she is not searching anymore.

{She found her mother
but not the one she was looking for.}

CLOSED FOR THE SEASON

Somewhere around October's end
depending on weather's grace
BDI's
closed for the season sign
pulls weatherbeaten shades
over work worn windows
tired benches like impromptu actors
on a winter stage
wait for their cue
to reassamble their lines
shadows of children's happiness
reverberate on urban bridge beams
the creamiest shakes in town
are just hibernating
to reappear when snow is gone
when welcome patterns of generations
return to fill the parking lot again
when benches resume
their proper posture
for tongues
to savor winter memories

{all summer long}

DISMANTLING A GARDEN

Frost comes as the grim reaper
to a garden in its splendid swing
sucking green hungrily
leaving plants limp and brown
draining life from once strong proud
zucchini now stooped wrinkled
blowing out last breath
from Cosmos
who resigns sadly and lets
flowers release petal by petal
blow-drying corn until
its leaves turn crusty and pasty
stray cucumbers
swollen and discolored in their demise
watermelon leaves
shrivel under its gaze

{Frost shows no compassion
no exception
relentless in its seasonal duty
as does life when winter bids autumn farewell.}

PART 4

Winter

OUTSIDE

Carefully constructed walls and posts
society assembles a social order
that determines where
the color and shape of lines are fixed
an invisible edge
that decides what is

{outside}

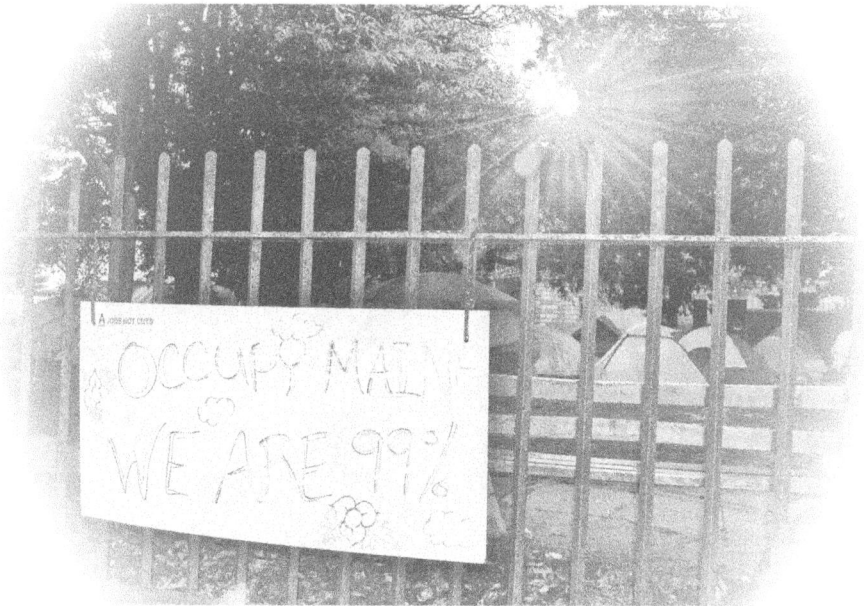

REQUIREMENT: YOUR CONSENT

(Eleanor Roosevelt quote on the Graffiti Wall at University of Winnipeg)

Angry words can maim
Harsh comments uttered disparagingly can disfigure but
although easier said than done it
requires consent

Rudimentary words roughly etched into
an irregular surface
although engraved with artistic modesty
can strengthen

                  {resolve}

MATCHING FLATWARE EXPECTATIONS

end of the day garage sale
a woman packs brown cardboard boxes with
things she doesn't need and no one else wants

what did you have I ask her amid boxes of books
freshly washed nightgowns and shirts
ensconced in a past life's detergent and laundry line

flatware peaks my interest and she digs it out from the bottom
of a faded box filled with her life's fragments
all matching

I tell her I have never had matching flatware
for $10 I buy our first set 26 years after
our other wedding gifts have gone threadbare and tired

> {What will happen
> with the miscellaneous flatware
> in our cupboards?
>
> In their humble diversity
> they still carry themselves
> with such elegance
> like my neighbor,
> who now lives in a lock down facility
> because her mind slipped
> on a patch of ice.}

SPRING CLEANING

Mariam sits in her state of repose
in an olive recliner
white sugar spun hair
pulled back into a soft bun
at the nape of her furrowed neck.

Her flowered smock
drapes loosely
over tired thin legs.
Leftover skin hangs droopily from her arms
but her eyes undulated with mischief
officious voice commands,
"Shine the silver, dust the cupboards."
In between instructions
she narrates yesterday's pictures
behind the cluttered pieces
takes me with her
on her journeys to India, England, Paraguay, Brazil.
Two grapefruit spoons accompany me home.
She doesn't need them anymore
in the winter of her life.

A few years later I see my friend
where she still sits in her olive recliner.
Her incoherent eyes
have forgotten my name.
Time has stolen the mischief
my yearly spring-cleaning of her cupboards forgotten

the globe of her mind shriveled.

> {When eating grapefruits I remember Mariam
> and savor every pocket of sweet juice
> because I don't know
> when time knocks for my memories.}

A WINTER DAY'S FAREWELL

Magical sunrays peek
into the living room picture window
at four in the afternoon
just after the bus drops us off
at the end of a winter's lane

a Milky Way galaxy inhabits
the living room
yet unnamed golden dust planets
spinning in orbit
diamond shard meteorites
hurdling through unknown textbooks
forming a halo over anyone that
walks through a rainbow
of sunny colors

{so quickly winter's dusk vanquishes light
gathering its forgotten sunbeams
in the apron of earth
only to scatter them freely again
at its four o'clock daily farewell}

HOMESPUN ICE RINK

When mercury
reached a steady well below freezing
my ever-thrifty Papa with my brothers
drove the old truck
with a promising water tank in back
a few miles
down the road to a farm pond
filled tank with generous water
more than charitable effort
to flood summer's garden
into an ice rink
which carefully collected unending days of winter
transformed them into perpetual adventure
hockey curling games
imaginative figure skating sessions
contrary to his parsimonious nature
Papa added a yard light
which supplied extended hours for night skating

> {In all those years of tedious work on
> the homespun rink
> I never once saw Papa on ice skates.
> Vicariously he reaped the benefits of his durable work
> by watching us skate
> listening to youth's laughter
> beckoning him from decades past.}

FROZEN POND IN THE HILLS

In a flourishing attempt to preserve
evocative memories
of skating and winter pleasure
New Mexico provided a challenging stage
for fulfilling winter recollections.

Year round we mentally marked ponds
on our winter calendar
for skating potentials.

One winter we discovered
a leftover pond in the hills
forgotten from fall's last downpour
water gathered, then ice
along with other
elapsed things

       {not even a box spring
       one odd boot
       yards of brown tape
       from someone's lost music
       all frozen into the pond
       like a static collage
       of strangers' refuse
       could muffle
       our stubborn determination
       to lasso a northern winter
       celebrating

marvelous wonder
of freezing temperatures
until our puck stuck in the box spring coils}

HOCKEY SYMPHONY

A freshly iced Canadian community rink
invites skaters
from hidden winter doors
One common bond
for the love of hockey
When enough players circle
flicking poised pucks against boards
a challenge to a friendly game
bids everyone to throw their sticks in the middle
One person with democratic hat covering eyes
sorts the sticks into two teams
in an affable way of avoiding
the lugubrious sting of being picked last
Players reclaim their sticks
and the dance of the hockey game starts
Graceful skaters stick in hand
interlace elegant passes
a penny whistle tune of
low and high thuds of puck
against stick and board
Skates swishing like finger cymbals clinging
Sticks crashing, cymbals clashing

> {A hockey symphony played by
> once upon a season friends}

READING A BOOK ON A MIDWINTER'S AFTERNOON

Winter farm life
without television
provided a paucity
of social life
but a wealth
of adventures through
windows of books.

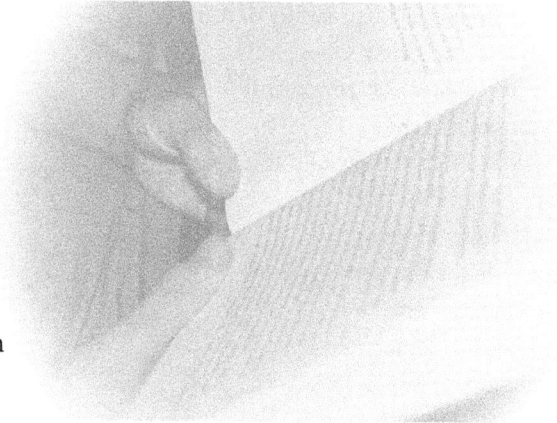

One winter snapshot
in my memory's album
shows me sitting
on a stuffed chair
snuggled tightly with my younger brother
each holding one side of a book
dissolving into another world
together
only on different pages of the trip

      {when one finished the final throws of the expedition
      we'd just switch places and start all over again}

TOBOGGANING

Our bountiful farm family of thirteen
owned one lonely toboggan
When winter covered the hill
across the rustic road
with enough toboggan promises
we all bundled up
taking jovial turns
pulling the one toboggan
up the reclusive hill
piling on like farm kittens
snuggled between jackets
so tight you forgot
where you started
where you ended

    {one congealed family
    interlocking pieces of one puzzle
    sailing down life's strategies
    only to pull apart
    separate slices
    at each trail's end}

LATE FOR SCHOOL

Mid winter wind nipped corners
of our small prairie farm house
forming topographical maps of
snowcapped icy mountains
on inside windowsills.

We listened to the radio static
expecting a snow day.
When no such anticipated announcement came
we bundled into our winter's best,
stomped through the rising snow drifts
to lane's end
to wait for the inevitable bus that came
filled with excited noses pressed against
steamy cold mystic windows.

Bus heavy with children
lumbered down gravel roads
where dunes encroached upon middle.

Finally on the Paddock road
drifts seized the entire road.
With one hopeful step on the gas
the bus sank its wheels into
snowdrifts' depth
only to be denied crossing
incapable of uttering the magic word.

To the bus driver's dismay we cheered
congratulating him on the winning goal
that would earn us a holiday from school
although just for an hour.

In search of a tractor
he stepped from the safety of the warm bus
into the angry storm outside
with our complete confidence
that he would return
with necessary help
to save us from
snow swirling in a mad frenzy
which he did of course
with a neighbor's tractor
not soon enough to catch the first bell.
Late for school came with a badge of honor
an accomplishment of great repute
to be talked about in winters to come.

{Remember when we got stuck on the Paddock road
and we were late for school.}

IN MEMORY OF DR. LOUIS P. SLOTIN

On Scotia Street
in a diminutive park hidden on the riverbank
a humble plaque
tells the brief story of Dr. Louis P. Slotin
Dec. 1, 1910-May 30, 1946
taken at the peak of his professional life
from 125 Scotia Street in Winnipeg
to Los Alamos in New Mexico
where as physicist/chemist he worked on the Manhattan Project
the birthplace of the atomic bomb
associated with grand scale damage and destruction
"Tickling the dragon" fission experiments
come with risks
an experiment gone wrong
Pandora's box opened too far
unleashed powers beyond human control
in late attempt to close the lid
he rescued his fellow scientists
from seeing
took the breach of radiation exposure
sacrificed his life
Contribution of radiation therapy
as treatment in modern medicine

{Two sides of a coin
one for life}

TWO BLUE SPRUCE

moved onto the farm when
I was about five
shyly they took their place
on each side of the front lawn
I towered over their two-foot stature
tussled their hair
they bowed respectfully to
their elders, the meticulous maples
that proudly lined the lane
commanded the tree politics
years wrapped their dogmatic rings
around those blue spruce
soon they rose
over me and the other stately trees

Years have gone by since the blue spruce came
from their hundred foot view now
they share their wisdom
as they stroke their scruffy beards
to all who stop and listen
the careful line of maples
with a few missing now
smiles like a jagged sculptured pumpkin
that company of trees witnessed
the coming and going of a family
they stayed there
rooted to the tradition of seasons
what wisdom they could impart

if only we understood their language

{My father planted two blue spruce seedlings in the front yard when he and his new wife, my mother, moved onto their first farmstead in Manitoba. I read this poem to my parents for their 50th wedding anniversary. A few years later, on the day that my father died in a personal care home in Paraguay, half way around the world from his original homestead near Rivers, Manitoba, one of the tall towering 50-foot blue spruce in the front yard, toppled to the ground. The blue spruce and my father arrived from opposite sides of the world, in the next season, on the same day.}

GOODBYE PAPA

after his body
is lowered into the ground
we take turns
digging spades
into rich soft memories
his life one with the land
seeds in spring furrows
wheat bending
to the melody of summer children
collecting the autumn harvest
for winter hibernation

{we say thank you
we will see you again on the other side
in the dimension we do not yet know}

EMPTY BENCH

In days gone by
we used to sit together
on a timeline.

      {Goodbye leaves empty spaces
      that were once filled with laughter and picnics.}

MORTALITY

Brittle leaves desert their secure attachment
to sail their first and last solo flight
into the unknown

A tired garden sighs
tomato plants thin and breakable
so quickly forget their
strong stems of succulent summer

A diffident forest
disrobed of its youthful green
lets season give way to season
without resistance

A young woman
breast cancer gnawing at
her children's birthdays
and each reclusive bite
sees eternity beckoning
but hangs on to everyday routines
with each breath and step

An unkempt lump with a crooked neck
on a bucolic roadside failed
to cross the yellow line
hit in the stride of life

A disheveled man with twisted limbs

follows detours in this world
forgotten there to suffer

A fresh cicada emerges from a
once sturdy shell that fulfilled its promise
A maple crowned in its green glory
flaming aspens
withered and bent tired oak
just a breath away from eternity
and

{a final welcome}

www.ingramcontent.com/pod-product-compliance
Lightning Source LLC
Chambersburg PA
CBHW071105090426
42737CB00013B/2498